Talk with Your Hands, Listen with Your Eyes

SPECIAL THANKS to Nancy Karkoska, a consultant in the field of deafness, and Pamela Martens, a Gallaudet University graduate, for their wonderful assistance and feedback.

Text copyright ©1993 by The Child's World, Inc.
All rights reserved. No part of this book may be
reproduced or utilized in any form or by any means
without written permission from the Publisher.
Printed in the United States of America.

Designed by Bill Foster of Albarella & Associates, Inc.
and Peter Hautman
Edited by Kristin Ellerbusch

Distributed to schools and libraries
in the United States by
ENCYCLOPAEDIA BRITANNICA EDUCATIONAL CORP.
310 South Michigan Ave.
Chicago, Illinois 60604

Library of Congress Cataloging-In-Publication Data

Ellerbusch, Kristin
Talk with your hands, listen with your eyes / written
by Kristin Ellerbusch.
p. cm.
ISBN 0-89565-974-3
1. American Sign Language — Juvenile literature.
2. Finger spelling — Juvenile literature.   I. Title.
HV2476.E45   1992
419 — dc20   92-24991
                                                    CIP
                                                    AC

Talk with Your Hands, Listen with Your Eyes

Written by Kristin Ellerbusch

Illustrated by Anastasia Mitchell

another Umbrella book

THE CHILD'S WORLD

Have you ever tried to watch TV without the sound?

Every day, people who are deaf have to watch people's lips move without being able to hear a voice. If you are deaf, you know what that is like.

Deafness doesn't spread from person to person—it isn't something you can catch. Yet every year, many people who were not born deaf become deaf from accidents or illness. That means some of us may be deaf some day, even if we aren't right now.

Once, over a hundred years ago, a man named Mason Cogswell had a little daughter who was deaf. At that time there were no schools in America where deaf children could be educated as they can be today, but Cogswell had heard of such a school in Europe. He loved his daughter Alice so much that he sent his neighbor, Thomas Hopkins Gallaudet, to England and then to France to learn about deafness so he could come back and educate Alice.

When Gallaudet came back to the United States, he brought with him a French sign-language teacher named Laurent Clerc. Together, the two men started what is now called the American School for the Deaf. In later years, Thomas Gallaudet had a son named Edward who started another deaf school—Gallaudet University. To this day, Gallaudet University is the world's only liberal arts college for the hearing-impaired people.

When Thomas Gallaudet and Laurent Clerc came to the United States from France, they brought with them a new language—a hand-signing language or "hand talk." This sign language that began in France evolved into what is now known as American Sign Language—or "Ameslan."

Ameslan (ASL) is the most commonly used language of the American deaf community—but even hearing people can learn it. Many colleges and universities teach Ameslan as a foreign language, but you don't have to wait until you go to college to learn it. *You* can learn to talk with your hands and listen with your eyes—and you can begin right now!

Letters

Signing words letter by letter is called fingerspelling. We're going to learn the alphabet first so you can fingerspell all the words you don't know how to sign.

Drop your arm to your side, then raise your hand to about shoulder level. Your palm faces out. As you learn each sign, compare the shape of your hand with the hand in this book. Finger for finger, make sure your handshape matches the picture.

When you sign the alphabet, you can use whichever hand works best for you—but don't keep switching. Right-handed signs are pictured here, so if you are left-handed you can practice in front of a mirror and compare your *reflection* with the pictures in the book.

A

B

C

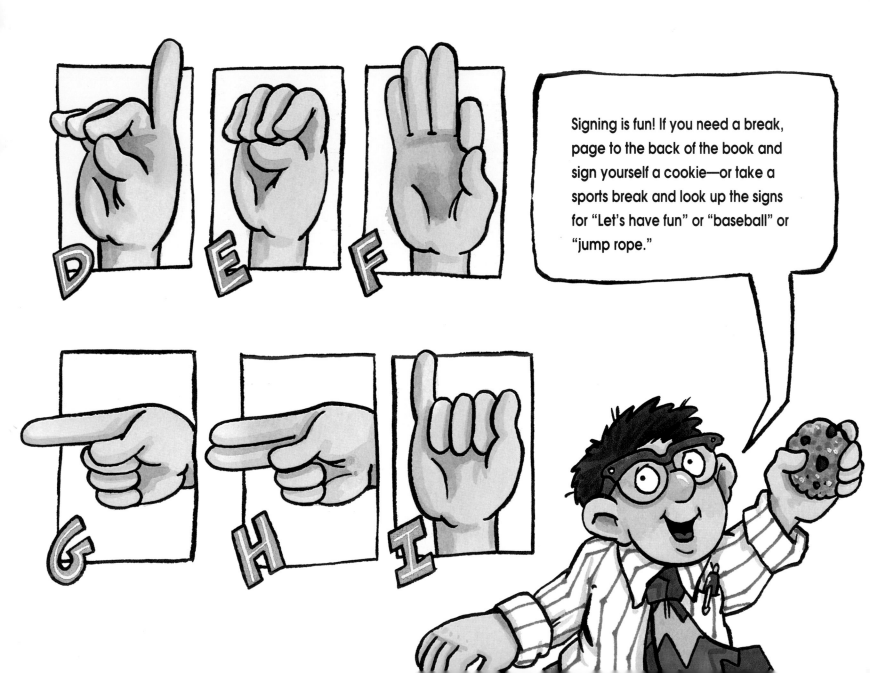

Signing is fun! If you need a break, page to the back of the book and sign yourself a cookie—or take a sports break and look up the signs for "Let's have fun" or "baseball" or "jump rope."

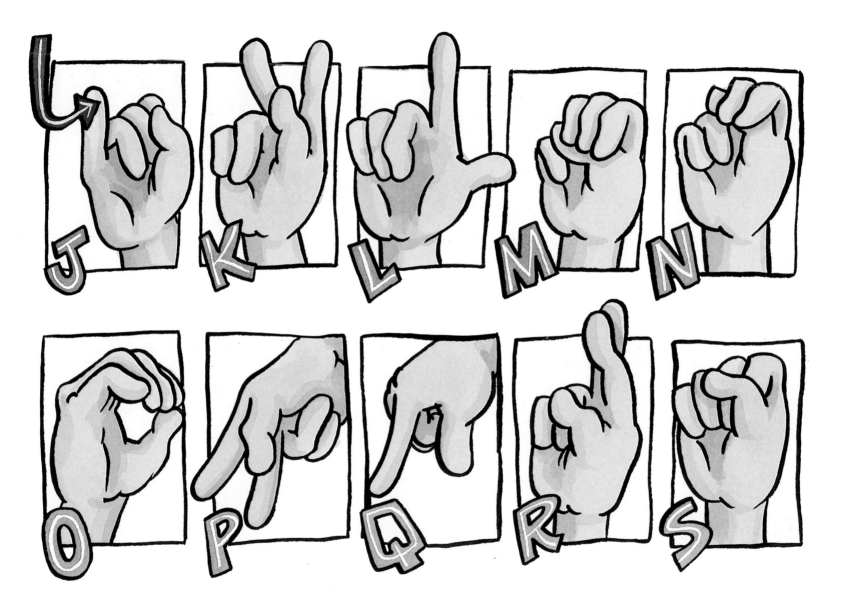

Once you know how to sign the alphabet, you can fingerspell any word in the dictionary—or at least any word you know how to spell. When you fingerspell, pause after each word. Look straight at the other person and speak the word as you sign it so your friend can also read your lips.

Numbers & Math Symbols

Colors

Fingerspelling is great! If you can fingerspell, you can say anything—but it's the slow way to do it. When I fingerspell I remind myself of a bug walking slowly up and down e-v-e-r-y s-i-n-g-l-e b-l-a-d-e of grass to get to a tree—when I could get there in seconds, if I only knew how to fly! When you learn to sign, you learn to fly.

If you know the alphabet, you already know almost all the color signs! Six of the colors are signed by simply waving the first letter of the word.

Wave the **Y** handshape.

Wave the **G**.

Wave **B**.

BROWN

This is another **B**, moved in a different direction.

PURPLE

Wave the **P** handshape.

PINK

Pink reminds us of lipstick. Form the **P** handshape again, but this time use your middle finger to stroke downward a couple times across your lips.

WHITE

This sign comes from the days of all-white shirts.

BLACK

Dark eyebrows help us remember black. Using the **one** handshape again, draw your pointer finger across your forehead above your eyebrows.

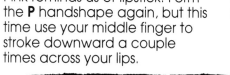

RED

Red reminds us of red lips. Using the **one** handshape, draw your pointer finger across your lips a couple times.

ORANGE

Put an open **O** up to your mouth and pretend you are squeezing orange juice from an orange.

People and Pets

Not all pets are listed here, but if you have a dinosaur named Pete, remember, you can always fingerspell him:

d-i-n-o-s-a-u-r n-a-m-e-d P-e-t-e

This two-part sign stands for "teach person."

Pretend you are pulling down the bill of a cap.

Trace a bonnet string with your thumb.

FAMILY

Use the **F** to form a family circle.

FRIEND

Interlocking fingers stand for interlocking hearts.

MOM

Notice that females are always signed at the jawline.

DAD

Males are signed off the forehead.

I (ME)

YOU

For pronouns, simply point to the person you want to refer to.

SNAP!

DOG

Slap your leg, then snap your fingers as if you were calling a dog.

CAT

Remember the cat's whiskers!

Lunch Time!

I don't know about you, but I'm getting hungry. Let's take a break! We'll use a few sign-language short cuts to get ourselves some fast food.

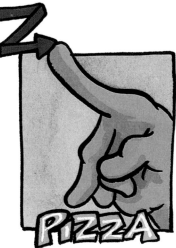

PIZZA

Form the **P** handshape, then write "Z" in the air.

HAMBURGER

Pretend you are forming a patty.

FRENCH FRIES

Sign the **F** twice.

COOKIE

Your hand shapes a round cookie

PEANUT

Scrape the peanut butter off the roof of your mouth

BUTTER

Pretend you are buttering bread

JELLY

Draw a **J** on your palm

SANDWICH

Your hands form the sandwich you pretend to eat

DRINK

Cup an imaginary glass in your hand and drink out of it.

SODA POP

Pretend you are pulling a cork out of a bottle—then pop it back in.

MILK

Pretend you are milking a cow.

WATER

Bring a **W** for "water" up to your lips.

WHAT'S YOUR FAVORITE ICE CREAM?

Your   favorite   ice cream?

Words You Can't Live Without

First we learned the alphabet and learned to fingerspell. Then we learned a few words. Are you ready for a conversation?

Keep in mind that a question is something you ask with your eyebrows. When you want to ask a question, just raise your eyebrows and look questioningly at the person you are signing to.

We're going to learn a few more sign-language short cuts here, so see if you can identify the words we leave out!

HELLO!

YES

Your hand nods like your head.

NO

PLEASE

THANK YOU

YOU'RE WELCOME

I'M SORRY!

EXCUSE ME

WHAT TIME IS IT?

TELEPHONE

MONEY

DEAF

LOVE

CLAP!

SCHOOL

BOOK

HOME

I HAVE TO GO TO THE R&R

"**R** & **R**" stands for restroom.

How are you doing? Are you getting the hang of these signs? See if you can figure out how to sign the following sentences.

I like pizza.

I love you.

What's your favorite book?

Thank you, Dad.

I'm sorry, Mom.

Sports

All the sport signs listed here, except football, mimic the action of the sport. If you know how to play the game, you'll know how to sign it!

LET'S HAVE FUN!

Verbs

Verbs are words that *do* something (*play* ball, *eat* pizza, *help* a friend). How many of these signs can you do?

Move your **V** fingers down an imaginary page.

When you write on imaginary paper, you won't make any mistakes.

Put your hands together as if you were praying.

Form the sign, then raise it up.

CAN

HAVE

KNOW

Curve your hand slightly and tap your fingers against your noggin.

WANT

GIVE

TAKE

SIT DOWN

Top fingers come down onto bottom fingers

LINE UP

Shhh!

Pedal with your hands!   Turn the steering wheel.

Holidays

Can you figure out how to sign the following sentences? You can fingerspell names if you don't know their signs.

Happy Birthday, Mom!

Happy Hanukkah, David! ("Happy Hanukkah, D-A-V-I-D!")

Merry Christmas, Dad!

What's your favorite Christmas cookie? ("Your favorite Christmas cookie?")

Use this sign before the name of each holiday

Top hand comes down onto bottom hand

HALLOWEEN

Point out the mask.

THANKSGIVING

CHRISTMAS

Notice the **C** handshape.

HANUKKAH

Remember the menorah.

NEW

Top hand lifts off
bottom hand

YEAR

Top hand circles
the bottom hand

BE

MY

VALENTINE

Tips for Easier Conversation

- If you want to start a conversation and can't get someone's attention, wave or gently tap the person on the shoulder.

- Make sure you have good lighting so the other person can see you clearly. Don't sign with your back to the window.

- Look straight at the person you are signing to. Speak word as you sign or fingerspell it, so the other person can read your lips.

- Sloppy signs are like mumbled words. If my signs aren't clear, you won't be able to understand me.

If you want to get to know someone, don't worry about making mistakes—just have a good time! If you accidently sign to a waitress that you want a hamburger instead of a cookie, you can eat your words and order dessert.